Eve, It's Adam. We Need To Talk.

Dating Issues For Men Women Probably Don't Know About But Should.

Darnell Lester, Jr.

iUniverse, Inc.
Bloomington

Eve, It's Adam. We Need To Talk.
Dating Issues For Men Women Probably
Don't Know About But Should.

iUniverse books may be ordered through booksellers or by contacting:

iUniverse
1663 Liberty Drive
Bloomington, IN 47403
www.iuniverse.com
1-800-Authors (1-800-288-4677)

ISBN: 978-1-4697-9731-1 (sc)
ISBN: 978-1-4697-9732-8 (e)

Printed in the United States of America

iUniverse rev. date: 3/6/2012

Dedication

This book is dedicated to the one woman I never had the opportunity to teach my life experiences – my baby sister. I miss you every day and you are still here living in my memory.

Lucretia C. Lester
December 25, 1979 – May 11, 1994

Contents

Introduction

These words are a culmination of experiences that my best friends, mutual friends, and I have encountered throughout our years of dating. This book includes many of the lessons we've learned along the way. We have seen and read about some of these topics before; while they may not necessarily be on the relationship radar of some women, they are most assuredly on the minds of men and definitely play a part in men's dating and relationship choices. The tone of these pages will range from serious introspection and advice to seemingly trivial and lighthearted issues, but issues important to some men nonetheless.

I don't claim to be a certified expert on relationships. In reality, who really and truly is? If we take the adage that "life is the best teacher" to be true, then the experiences on these pages have taught my friends and I lessons that we would like women to understand. Even if they don't fully understand these experiences, they should at least think about them when dealing with dating and relationships.

What exactly are these things that men talk about when it comes to dating and relationships? The issues that affect men's dating decisions are as diverse as the types of relationships between men and women.

It is my intention to show others that men too are complex and there is more than one issue that concerns us in our so-called "one-track mind" when it comes to dating.

This book is not about female-bashing or putting all women in one category. This book seeks to give women some insight into men's minds and a few other issues that matter to men in order to start and maintain a healthy relationship. Granted, the differences between men and women frustrate both of us, but they also draw us to each other. In my opinion we do not talk about these differences enough.

Ultimately, the objective of this book is to start a healthy dialogue. Now the question that should be asked is, since the two of you are talking, are you just hearing each other or are you truly listening? There is a difference.

Left And Right Brain

I tend to look at some relationships and classify them in a "left-brain, right-brain" fashion. Science tells us that the left brain controls a certain number of our body's functions, and the right brain controls a vastly different set of body functions. In order for the brain to comprehend complex situations, constant communication must occur between the two hemispheres. Without this constant communication, the body is left in a confused, incapacitated state. Many relationships have the same problem because there is no communication between the relationship's left brain (the truth) and the relationship's right brain (what we want to hear). Simply put, you can't have it both ways because the breakdown in communication in the relationship will become evident.

My friends and I are often frustrated by the catch-22 that is associated with telling the truth when we meet some women. You would think telling the truth to a woman would be commended (and expected), but I cannot count the number of times men have been looked upon with scorn because the actual truth was not the "expected truth."

For example, if we are having a discussion, what I say to you is what I mean. Please don't try to read anything more into it. At that point, it is your decision whether or not to accept what is being said. Some women respect when a man respects her feelings enough to tell the truth and not lie to get somewhere or something from her. Even though he might not give the answer she is expecting, she respects him for letting her decide whether to be a part of a type of relationship that she did not want before deeper emotions become involved.

I must admit I have not always thought about approaching women and revealing my intentions to them. In my fresh-out-of-college years, I definitely played the game of telling women what I thought they wanted to hear to get what I wanted. I had no regard for their feelings that may have been affected when my true intentions were revealed. This led to so much self-imposed stress, and it destroyed would-be friendships.

That all changed in 1997. I was at a bar with my best friend and as usual, we were talking about our situations with women. I told him how I, once again, had to go through an elaborate story with a woman I was "dating." At that time in my life, dating really meant someone I was sleeping with. I was dating more than one woman, but I was telling each of them that they were the only one. Needless to say, it was a grind trying to hide the secrets and keep the date nights straight. After thirty minutes of my ranting, he said something that changed me forever. I still live by his words to this very day. He said, "Dee, I can tell how to keep it all together." I replied, "How?" He said, "Man, just tell them the truth." I looked at him as if he needed to be committed to an institution for unstable people.

He could tell there was much doubt from me, but he explained his rationale. In hindsight, it is some of the best advice I have ever received. He basically explained that if you are honest, you don't find yourself lying to begin the relationship and continually lying to keep the story intact.

It is definitely much easier to remember the truth about what happened than it is to remember a lie about what happened. In many cases, lies become an unnecessary, elaborate production with many unnecessary players. I can remember times that, in order to keep a story intact, I recruited the help of my friends to perpetuate the story. I would review in detail with them what I had told the lady I was dating. I would even drill them with questions that she might ask to see if their responses were feasible! Sounds crazy, right? Yeah, I know. I created a lot of unnecessary work, right? Right.

Once I began telling women the truth, the conviction of lies was no longer upon my head. I was looking for friendships—and, yes, some with benefits. I knew that I had presented her with the option to say yes or no in establishing a friendship with me. And if, at some point, she became frustrated with the situation, my conscience was clear and absolved. And that clarity of mind and soul alone was immeasurable.

With all that being said, the catch-22 of telling the truth remained. What do you do when you tell the truth and someone still hears what they want or expect to hear from you?

On talk shows and in books, many women say they just want honesty from a man. They want him to put all his cards on the table or—my personal favorite— play no games! Before looking at the last statement and saying, "Yeah, that's exactly what I am talking about!" be sure to take a long, hard look within and ask if that is truly what you want. More importantly, ask yourself how you would handle it if you were told the truth but not the way you expected to hear it. Be sure to temper yourself for the harshness of the truth. The truth is a very strong medicine; many times, it is an acquired taste. Sometimes the truth hurts, bottom line. But there is truth, pun intended, to the adage that the bitter elixir heals the soul.

I met a very attractive, interesting woman during a party I was throwing for my friends. We talked and exchanged numbers at the end of the night. Over the next few weeks, we began to talk on the phone, and finally I invited her over to my home for dinner. As the saying goes, "one thing led to another," and we ended up in the bedroom. There was so much heavy kissing and touching. The sexual tension became enormous, but before anything went any further, I stopped and asked, "What is it that you are looking for?" She said, "What is it that you are looking for, Darnell?" I told her that I was not looking for a serious relationship with anyone, and I was "dating" other people at that time. I asked her if she was okay with this, and she told me she was. We had "nice, hot, lovely relations" that night. We went out from time to time and continued to share our bedrooms but things began to change.

I began to see signs that her feelings may have been changing from having a friendship to wanting much more. I sat down with her and reiterated that I was still not looking for a serious relationship but pointed out that I could see things were possibly changing for her. I even suggested that we stop having those "lovely relations," to keep things from becoming even more complicated. She told me that she understood how I felt and that ceasing the "lovely relations" would not be necessary. She said that she was okay with our situation. Looking back at that situation, it seems as though she was betraying her heart and telling me what she thought I wanted to hear—instead of what she was really feeling. All the while, I was under the impression that we were in agreement about the status of our relationship.

Months later, she admitted that her feelings had deepened and she wanted a more serious, committed relationship. I told her that the type of relationship I wanted had not changed and that I did not want a serious relationship. She became extremely frustrated and could not understand why I did not feel the way she felt or why I wanted to continue to see other people. The answer was as simple: I did not want that type of relationship with anyone at that point in time.

Our dialogue continued for many months, leaving us both even more frustrated with each ensuing conversation. I even went so far as to ask my best friend to speak with her to see if hearing the same answer from a different voice would make a difference. Although you don't want to have too many people involved in your situations, there are times when a third voice can be a valuable mediator. Using a mediator can sometimes be the best method for dealing with relationship issues because there are no emotions involved that may impair the conversation. She told him that she knew I wanted to be with her, but I would not admit it. She said she was going to show me that was the case. Once again, it was a situation of someone hearing what she wanted to hear instead of what was being said.

The unfortunate situation reached a crossroad when I accepted a traveling position in a city an hour and a half away. I would periodically travel home to take care of business in North Carolina. On one particular occasion, one of her friends apparently saw my car in the area and told her that I was in town. I had no intention of telling her that I was coming home that weekend because I did not want to have another one of our stalemate conversations.

However, I had made plans to go out with another young lady that evening. I was awaiting her arrival at my home as I was unpacking my car. In the midst of unpacking, Sheila, the woman I had been having these "discussions" with, showed up at my door unannounced. This was a major no-no. We had repeatedly talked about it and agreed how disrespectful it was, but she was doing exactly that.

We talked—or should I say borderline yelled at each other—and she asked me what I was doing home. I countered by asking what was she doing at my home unannounced. She told me that she had been in the neighborhood and wanted to see if I was home. The only problem with her story is that she lived at least thirty minutes away. While Sheila and I were talking, the young lady that I had made plans with showed up at my house. Sheila began to lose it and said repeatedly, "Oh, so this is the bitch you want?"

Sheila was crying, screaming, and making a complete scene – with my help of course. After seeing this "conversation," the other young lady refused to get out of her car. I was irate. I told Sheila never to come to my house again and to lose my number. My emotions ranged from anger to embarrassment to disgust. Sheila eventually left—but not without leaving an embarrassing situation for everyone at my home.

As life would have it, a few months later, work called me away to another state. I would be six hours away from North Carolina. Even with everything that we had gone through, I continued to keep some communication with Sheila. One day, she called me at work. To this day, I still do not know how she obtained my number but during the conversation, we revisited the relationship issue. I explained that I was six hours away, in a new city, meeting new people and a long distance relationship was out of the question. Once again my answer was transposed and distorted into what she wanted to hear and not what was being said.

Once again, we became frustrated over the fact that she could not understand why I did not want a committed relationship, especially one that was long distance. This time, I was not willing to relive any more of the frustration; the constant repetition had become as standard as a verse of Shakespeare's finest. A decision had to be made and I made it. I decided to end all communication and ties with her. As drastic as that sounds, it had to be done because your sanity and staying true to yourself—and the other person—outweigh any consequences of the fallout.

Can We Talk?

A nother thing that men would like women to understand is that sometimes a conversation at a bar or favorite nightspot is just that—a conversation with no further intentions. It may be hard to believe, but men sometimes like to have conversations for the sake of conversations.

Intellect is attractive, and from time to time, we seek it out too. Now, I am not blind to the fact that many men go to nightspots with the intention of meeting a woman to engage in "other activities" but do not turn your head to the fact that just as many women have the same intention. It is just something that is not spoken of that often.

Step into my dream world for a second and ponder this thought. You are enjoying your ultra cosmopolitan in a bar, and a gentleman steps up to you. He says, "Is this seat taken?" When you tell him that it's not, he sits down. You engage in the obligatory small talk that leads to more in-depth conversation, but somewhere along the line you think, *hey, this guy really has something to say*. You find yourself laughing and having a good time throughout the conversation.

After thirty minutes or an hour, he says, "It was very nice meeting you and I enjoyed talking to you." When he walks away, do you wonder why he didn't ask for your number or try to make a move on you? Could it be because you are under the impression that any man who talks to you when you're out on the town automatically wants to sleep with you? If so, that is not always true.

I have seen instances where men have sat down and tried to talk to women. However, before he can say two words, there is a preconceived notion that takes form, and he is shut out immediately. My humble, nonprofessional, but experienced advice would be not to let the "only-thing-men-are-after" mentality halt the opportunity to meet an interesting person. Believe it or not, you might have liked him or wanted to get to know more about him. For all you know, the man that you have been asking God for just sat down—and you turned him away.

Adam and Eve

How can men have sex with so many different women and seem as though they have little or no emotional ties to them? Have you ever asked yourself that question or had discussions about it in your sisters' circles? The simple answer, in my opinion, is that women are primarily emotional beings, and men are physical beings. In most cases, it is easier for a man to separate sex and love. As much as you may hear that women can just have sex with no emotion, which in some cases is true, the number of those women seem to be far less than the number of men. It seems as though it is the nature of men to think more on an analytical and physical level rather than on an emotional level. Even if a woman starts out in a relationship that is purely physical—and satisfying to her—as the sexual relationship continues and more time is spent with that person, a strong emotional attachment tends to develop.

I will say that all men are not just emotionless creatures—even though some folks may beg to differ. Women often say, "How can you not feel any emotional attachment for a woman when you have been with her for a while?" The answer is that sometimes you can be in a physical relationship with someone where the two of you just click. You are able to bring out those long-thought desires in each other. Just as with anything, you can develop chemistry with someone—even if it is only on a physical level. Chemistry is usually one of the things that you can't explain, but you know it exists. For example, have you ever been in a physical relationship with someone you knew you would never date seriously, but you kept the person around because the sex was incredible? Answer truthfully. As much as you may not want to admit it, I would venture that a number of you would answer yes.

The problems arise when you and your partner do not take the time to make "emotional pit stops" in the relationship. Emotional pit stops are what I call the conversations that the two of you need to have at various points in the relationship to see where each of you stands on an emotional level.

It is imperative in a relationship that is based on a "friendship with an understanding," both people have the same understanding about the status of the relationship. Confusion arises when one person's feelings have changed, but nothing is said to the other person. The one with the change in feelings makes the assumption that his or her partner's feelings are in line with their own.

Here is a word of advice. Don't wait until you are too emotionally tied to a person to discuss how you feel. Failing to do so will only bring about more hurt and anger. It will manifest when you can't understand how you and this person have been "together" for so long but they still want to see other people and don't feel the same as you do. The assumption of mutual emotions and attachments cannot be made. You must discuss it. Otherwise, it is unfair to the other person—and, more importantly, to you.

Now That We've Had Sex, What Do We Do Next?

Now that we have had sex, where do we stand? That's the point exactly—where do we stand? As much as having sex with someone may change a relationship, it does not necessarily make it a committed relationship by default. People cannot make the assumption that they become exclusive once they and their partner have had sex—especially if they have not discussed it at any length. Men often hear this frustration from women who have gone through this scenario with the men in their lives.

The boundaries of your relationship have to be set before you have intimate relations. I am not naïve to believe that you always have the ability to stop in the heat of the moment to have a heart-to-heart conversation. Life is never that perfect or simple. In the case of spontaneous sexual combustion, you must sit down afterward to discuss the boundaries of your relationship if you have not beforehand.

You cannot assume that once you have begun an intimate relationship, your partner is not going to have any other intimate relationships—or stop any others that he or she may have started before you met. This, more than anything else, is the reason why you *have* to talk. I will admit to the fact that, for the majority of women, giving themselves to someone is more than just a physical thing. Many times, it involves emotions and underlying tones of exclusivity. But once again, just because that is your view of what having sex with someone involves, you can't assume that the other person's view is the same as yours if you have not had any discussions about the matter. As much as you would like to get upset about a guy or girl seeing other people after the two of you have "known" each other biblically speaking, if you don't set the boundaries for what you expect, there are really no grounds to be upset with the other person.

I met a beautiful young lady one evening when I was not planning on going anywhere originally. It was a spur-of-the-moment thing that we all have from time to time. As I walked into the club and strolled over to my usual posting spot, she walked past me. From that moment, she had my full attention; I found out that I had hers when she came over to say hello. We exchanged numbers and began talking on the phone. We talked about everything under the sun, including sex, and she told me that she was at a point in her life where she had to be in an exclusive relationship with someone before she could give herself to them. I, on the other hand, told her that I was not looking to get into an exclusive relationship at that particular time because I had ended a relationship less than a month earlier that had left a few scars. I also let her know I was listening to what she was saying. I told her that I would respect her wishes and not pressure her into any situation.

Everything about us was new. We were beginning to go through the stage of figuring out if there really was something between us. As fate would have it, a couple months or so after we met, the sexual tension generated from kissing and touching reached a level that took us to the point of no return. Afterward, we agreed that we might have moved a bit too fast since we had discussed it earlier, but we could not take it back. There could be no do-over.

A few weeks later, I went back to the spot where I had met her to have a few drinks and people-watch. I came across a young lady who had just moved to the city and was celebrating her birthday. Even though it was her birthday, she was feeling as though she was the third wheel because her girlfriend had her guy friend with her. The birthday girl had left her man at home because he did not want to go out to celebrate.

Ladies, I will fess up and apologize for the stupidity that this man placed upon my gender. Men, I don't care what you are doing or don't feel like doing; you never tell your lady that you don't want to go out on her birthday. Especially, knowing how important dates are to women. Amen, ladies?

She and I began to talk and as the night moved along, she asked me if I wanted to dance. I was so obliged to do just that. We danced until the obligatory slow jam that some clubs play at the end of the night came on. I saw no reason to stop dancing—and neither did she.

We were dancing very closely to the melodic sounds of the Purple One—Prince. We were singing the song in each other's ears as best we could and holding on to each other as we sang. When the club lights came on, she asked if I would walk her to her car. Being the Southern gentleman that I am, I did just that. As I was walking to her car, my mobile phone began to ring. Lo and behold, it was Lisa, the lady that I had met just a few weeks earlier. She asked me who I had been dancing with and why I had been dancing so close to her.

I immediately began to look around as if I was a deer caught in the hunter's scope, but I did not see her. She told me that her girlfriends had seen me on the dance floor and called her. She asked, "Who was that? What were you doing with her?" I explained that I had just been dancing, and there was nothing wrong with dancing because we were not boyfriend and girlfriend in the first place. Now, before you begin to think that I was trying to make a move on the birthday girl, I wasn't. That assumption would be far from the truth. Since her boyfriend did not come out for her birthday, I wanted her to at least have a pleasant memory of her birthday. Is that so wrong?

Lisa continued to ask questions, but I told her that it was something that I was not going to discuss at that moment. I told her that we could talk about it when we were not in the heat of the moment.

Later that week, Lisa came over to my house and started with the questions again. I realized that her questions and comments were the type that someone would hear if they were in committed relationship. When the conversation became heated, I realized that we needed to have an "emotional pit stop." I asked exactly what her friends had told her about that night. After she gave me their version, I gave her the true version because there was absolutely nothing to hide in the first place.

I also reiterated that we were not in a committed relationship and that her actions made me feel as though she was treating our relationship as a committed one, even though we had not discussed it since our last talk. She admitted that now she did want the commitment, but I told her that I was still not ready to make that move. Although the sexual tension was enormous for the next several weeks, we kept our pact until, and if, we decided to be committed to each other.

Common-Law Relationships

L adies, I want to acknowledge one time when men put ourselves at fault when we begin spending more time with you. It is a catalyst for some of the confusion that we have in our relationships. It is called a common-law relationship.

Here's a little background on the common-law relationship. Some states have laws that say you are legally married if you and your significant other have lived under the same roof conducting your lives in a way that is "marriage-like" for a stated number of years. Depending upon the state, common-law couples have all the rights and privileges of a couple married with all the pageantry and regalia of a wedding. In other words, the law figures that if you are going to play married, then you may as well be married.

The same type of situation happens in some dating relationships. I have been as guilty of this common-law relationship as any other guy out there. Once upon a time, I was in a relationship with a female and in the beginning, we both stated that we did not want a "boyfriend-girlfriend" relationship because we both had recently come out of committed relationships and wanted to take a break from that. We started going out, did things together, and enjoyed each other's company. We wanted to continue our "noncommittal" relationship and decided it was okay if we became physical with one another. It was a friendship with an understanding, so to speak.

We continued going out, and it progressed to a point where I would stay at her house maybe once or twice a week, and she would do the same at my home. As time passed, we had discussions that we would not date other people while we were together. However, if we wanted to make that choice to do so, out of respect for the other person, we would let the other person know.

As the months passed and we spent more and more time with each other, I began to spend more nights at her house. We were together at least six out of seven nights, but we were not in a "boyfriend-girlfriend" relationship. Or were we? Looking back in hindsight, I realize that we had become boyfriend and girlfriend by common law. We did everything that would be seen as a committed relationship, but we both wanted to deny the fact that we were "together" and a relationship like that can only lead to one thing: confusion.

So, I have some advice for the fellas. Don't play "committed relationship" if you don't want to be in one. It saves so much time, confusion, and hurt because your actions contradict your words. We are usually judged by our actions more than by our words because our actions generally don't lie.

Just The Way You Look Tonight

As most mental-health professionals would say, the admission of denial is always the first step toward recovery. There are some of us out there who need recovery desperately.

I've heard people say, "When I meet someone, I am attracted to their personality more than by how they look." or "Looks are not what attract me to someone." Please be honest with yourself and the rest of us and admit that your statement is so far from the truth that it is virtually unbelievable. You mean to tell me that when you look at someone, you have that extrasensory perception that allows you to look into their head or heart and see their attractive personality? I think not. Would it be safe to say that you are attracted to something physically appealing about them initially? Because that is all there is to know about someone until you actually have a conversation with them. Until then, you initially are attracted to some physical feature about them. Maybe it's their eyes, their smile, the way they walk across the room, or a certain look that lets you know they are interested. Who knows, after sitting down for a glass of wine and talking with them, you may find that they have the most unattractive personality.

How many times have you heard—or even said yourself—that someone was physically attractive, but his or her personality made him or her ugly? Physical attraction is the initial draw to someone that makes us want to know more about them. It gives you butterflies in your stomach when they pass by and smile at you. It is what draws you to them. Without that initial physical attraction, there can't be any type of emotional or personal attraction that we all seek, which ultimately makes or breaks any relationship we choose to enter.

If there is any doubt in what I am saying, there is a really simple test that can be applied to prove the point. It is as easy as your friendly neighborhood online dating service. Go to any of them and create a search for all the profiles that match your wants in someone but, do not have any pictures. Read what they have to say. Find a few that attract you and strike up a friendly conversation with them through e-mail.

Continue that conversation for a while before you ask for a picture. The odds are fifty-fifty that the person will turn out to be someone you are physically attracted to. If the person is attractive to you, then great! You have found your combination of looks and personality. However, what if the person wasn't physically attractive to you? What do you do then? Do you stick by your words that you are more attracted to a person's personality than their looks? I would bet that there would be some change in the current standing of the conversation or relationship. If I am wrong, let me know about it.

It's Just The Little Things That You Do

Ladies, the little things that you do in preparation for an evening out make a man appreciate the beauty of a woman and the detail she takes in looking beautiful.

For me, and other men to whom I have spoken, it is an indicator of the type of woman we feel you are. For example, an attractive woman approaches a guy who is out for a night on the town. As she gets closer, her sexy glide is entrancing. She draws him in even more with the formfitting dress that accentuates every curve of her body. He imagines himself later using his hands to retrace the curves that he's just seen. He does his best to make eye contact with her.

When he smiles at her, she smiles back. He makes his approach with a simple hello and speaks his name. As he stretches his hand out to make her acquaintance, she obliges. He looks at her fingers and sees chipped nail polish, un-manicured nails, or dirty nails. At that moment, the image of his exquisite woman vanishes into thin air as if it had been a dream. Ladies, men are physically very observant, as you well know. One of the first things that my friends and I pay attention to when we meet a woman is her hands and feet. The theory is simple: If she always takes the time to have manicured hands and pedicured feet, she pays attention to the details and cares about her appearance. It is a major indicator for us.

It is not hard to do. Just take a little time to have them done. If you can do it yourself, then do that. If not, I am sure you are aware that there are nail shops everywhere. They are like a liquor stores—you can find them on almost every corner these days. Go visit one. But when you do, please, please, please make sure you match colors. A "two-toned" woman is not that appealing; and it's somewhat of a turnoff. What is a two-toned woman? A two-toned woman is a lady who may have a French manicure and painted feet. What is that? That is not sexy. Choose one: color or no color. You decide. All we ask is that you make a choice and apply that choice to your hands and feet. Personally, there is nothing sexier than seeing a nicely dressed woman with French manicured hands and French pedicured feet. It adds an air of simplicity and sophistication. A hint of subtlety is indeed sexy.

The "Undies"-Niable Truth

This is something that many ladies already know. To those who do, we thank you for understanding. But for those who don't know or may not have thought of it before, understand this rule. Repeat after me: Wearing the right underwear is important.

There is nothing like seeing a woman in a formfitting skirt or dress that accentuates every curve of her body. As she passes by, we admire her even more, and then we see it—the unthinkable, unforgivable "granny panties." At that moment, we are immediately turned off. That sight, ladies, is so unattractive. The line of the "T" is all we want to see if you are going to wear them. There are certain types of material that do not work well with full underwear, especially when we can see panty lines or—even worse—bunched panties; major turnoff.

You don't like them, you say? If you have tried them and don't like them, then okay. But if you say that you don't like them and have never tried them, I would say to try them before making a decision. Isn't that what we would tell our kids about eating certain vegetables? How would you know if you haven't tried it? Want to test this theory? If you have a man in your life, try the following experiment with him:

Go to Victoria's Secret or your favorite lingerie store. Find a pair of thong or g-string underwear that you like. Go home and slip them on without your man knowing. At some point, go into your bedroom and come up with a reason for him to come into the bedroom too. As he enters the room, have your back facing the door. Wait for him to enter the room. As he enters, listen for a reaction. When you hear it, turn around and look at his face. I promise you will see a man who wants you more than anything at that moment.

Ideally, as the night moves into lovemaking, try to be conscious of the amount of times he touches your bum, comments the next day about what you had on last night, and says how sexy you looked in them. Then, for the rest of the week, go back to wearing the granny panties. See how much he talks about the thong or g-string the rest of the week and how much he was turned on by seeing you in them. Remember the night that you wore them and how passionate it was. And then tell me if thongs—or better yet, the lack thereof—do not make a difference. Remember that we need our visuals.

For Me?

There are some old-fashioned traditions regarding relationships that I think should never change. For example, a man should always be the one to find his wife. He should always ask her parents for her hand in marriage. However, at this particular time, the rules for dating have changed. More and more, we find couples who began by dating on the Internet, speed dating, or joining local single circles. One current dating change that men would like to see utilized more often is showing a man that he is appreciated from time to time. Yes, there. I said it. Go against the grain sometimes. Take a chance. Walk up to him and tell him he is attractive—and you did not want anything more than to tell him that.

Instead of waiting for him to buy you a drink, if you are interested in meeting him—or if the two of you are out on the town—buy him a drink. He will definitely look at you in a different, and most appealing, light. You have no idea what affect that can have on a man. Trust me. I remember the first time a lady offered to buy me a drink. I remember it as if it happened yesterday. Maybe it was yesterday, but she walked over and said, "Excuse me. What are you drinking?"

I said, "Excuse me?"

She said, "What is that in your glass?"

I told her what I was sippin' on, and she walked up to the bar. Being in the mind-set of the usual path that conversation takes, I was expecting to see her sippin' on the same thing when she stepped away from the bar. When she turned around, she had *two* drinks in her hand. As she extended the glass to me, I said, "That's for me?"

She said it was, and then she asked me my name. She told me it is was nice to meet me and walked away. Folks, I had just been gamed by my own game and ooooh, it felt so good. Needless to say, I looked for her later, and we struck up a conversation. I had to let her know how impressed I was by the fact that she had decided to buy me a drink. I liked that she did not mind being a little different, and she was not afraid to make the first move.

To carry that a bit further, I've found that some men have a real issue with a lady that will not offer to pay for dinner or anything else during a night out on the town. The key word here is *offer*. Admittedly, I am from the old school when it comes to dating. If I ask a woman out, I expect to cover most, if not all, of the expenses for our evening. But, if *you* ask me out and expect me to pay for everything, you can pretty much guarantee that it will be our first and last date.

I went on a few dates with a woman I really enjoyed spending time with but eventually our friendship ended on not the greatest terms. I first saw her in the gym. One evening after a nice workout, I asked if she would go out with me. She said yes. Since I asked her out, I would be covering everything. And I did.

As we continued to go out on dates, I noticed that she never once opened her purse to even purchase a pack of gum. And that, my friends, was a major problem and sticking point for me. But here was the kicker. She once asked me out to the movies, but as we approached the ticket counter, she asked for two tickets—and proceeded to step away! I looked at her with a somewhat befuddled look and said to myself, "What the hell?" She was waiting for me to pay for a date that *she* had invited *me* on. I paid but that, my friends, was the last straw. Somehow I intentionally erased her number by mistake from my phone and my memory.

Later, when she noticed that I was not calling her or asking her out anymore, she asked why. In the midst of our conversation; I said, "How is it that I pay on a date when you asked me out?"

She said "I never pay when I go out. I feel that I don't have to pay."

I told her that we had a problem. She wanted to try to tell me that she did not have any money to do those things, but I would see her at places where she was definitely spending money. Don't get me wrong. It is not all about the money. Actually, it isn't about the money at all. It is about appreciation. I promise that if you take it upon yourself and offer to pick up the tab a few times, you will find that he will begin to grab the tab before you even have an opportunity to see the ink dry. All we are asking is that you make the offer. Nine times out of ten, we will say, "That's okay. It's on me." Just make the offer. It can carry you places in the minds of men.

The Female Puzzle—Putting The Pieces Together

Ladies, have you ever asked yourself how is it that a man can date more than one woman at the same time? Why is it that he cannot find everything he needs in one woman?

Today I have an answer—or shall I say a theory—that may shed some light on those questions. The answer is that everyone, male and female, has the ideal person with whom they would like to spend their time—and, if things go well, possibly start a relationship. That ideal person will have certain qualities that we seek and find attractive. However, we don't often find all of those qualities wrapped up in one beautiful package. Sometimes we find certain qualities of our ideal woman in one woman and other qualities in another. That is why we may date more than one woman at the same time. Combining the different qualities or characteristics of our ideal woman in more than one lady creates our ideal woman, at least in theory. Before you say that is a bunch of garbage, let's dig a little deeper.

My ideal woman must have a sense of humor and an adventurous nature, be able to carry on a good conversation, love to travel, and be a kid at heart. I also like an independent woman who does not need all of my attention in order to be happy—someone who can watch a ballgame or go to a sporting event with me. As much as I would like to believe that I can find all of those qualities in one woman, the chances of finding my "ideal her" are very slim. This leads to the following rationale for some men. "Until I am ready to find—and settle down with—the one woman who I think will be the mother of my children, I will date the women that make up the whole of my ideal woman."

Believe it or not, ladies, some of you may have been in this same situation once or twice. Whether or not you dated them or had them as friends, you probably have been in this "puzzling" situation. For example, you may know someone who is just the most physically attractive man in the world. If we let you tell it, when he *brings* it to you, the earth moves, you hear birds singing, and he puts you in a drunken, body-pulsing state of being. But as soon as you try to have a little mental stimulation through intelligent conversation with him, he has no conversation whatsoever. He is good to look at, and that is about all there is to him. However, for some reason, even though you could not see yourself in a relationship with this man in a million years, you can't let him go because the things he does to your body are just amazing—and, dare I say, addictive.

Another guy might be the greatest listener in the world. For any problem, you can call him, and he is there—regardless of the hour—to listen to what you have to say. If asked, he will offer advice for the situation. Even though he is the one guy that understands you and will listen to what you have to say, he is in no way anyone that you would be attracted to physically. You know the man I am talking about, ladies. The "he is a great guy, but I just don't see him in that way" guy.

After you have been sexed like crazy—and told the guy who listens to you about it—you call up the guy who has the culture and adventurous spirit that stimulate your mind. He is the one who likes to do the things that are out of the ordinary. He might like to go boating, try new restaurants, or go to a play or a concert. If your ideal man is someone who listens to you when you need an available ear, someone who is adventurous and active, or someone who can sex you like crazy, those three men would make up your ideal man.

And that is all some men are saying, ladies. Until they are ready for a solid, committed relationship, they might create their ideal woman with more than one woman.

Interracial Dating Isn't Just A Black-and-White Issue

I grew up in a very small, rural area of South Carolina. We had to travel twenty miles to the local high school, and one local pool was still segregated as late as 1994. The cover was that it was a private pool for "members only," but the entire community knew that the members were those who were not of a sub-tropical origin, if you get my drift. With that being said, interracial dating was nearly unheard of in our community. At the very least, it was as undercover as if it had been a covert CIA operation.

During my college years in South Carolina, I mainly dated African-American women. Even though I would see an attractive lady of another race, I would not approach her mainly because of the stigma that was associated with interracial dating in the rural South. However, a strange thing began to happen as the years progressed.

After I graduated from college, I moved to Charlotte, North Carolina, and my mind-set about dating began to shift 180 degrees. The culture of the city was different from what I was accustomed to. Even though Charlotte was located in the heart of the South, the people who lived there were mainly transplants from more progressive areas of the country. These people had more open mind-sets and views on dating that changed my mind-set as well. In hindsight, I can say it was definitely for the best.

My best friend and I began to frequent places that were not considered predominately "urban" establishments, and we began to talk to women who did not look like us. These women were some of the most interesting people we met. Even though these women did not look like us, some of them had the same interests as we did. We did receive some opposition to our newfound dating philosophies from some of my people. Some of them even stopped talking to us and had negative things to say, but their actions actually helped us. Their actions allowed us to weed out the people in our lives who truly did not have our best interest at heart. In the end, it comes down to who makes you happy. I don't think the Lord is going to stand at the pearly gates and keep someone out of heaven for dating someone who is not of their own race.

We are all God's people, aren't we? Emotions are not based on skin color. Personalities are not based on skin color. If we believe we begin a relationship with someone mainly because of their personality, how can we close ourselves off to a person who may not look like us? We may have cultural differences that make us who we are, but trying to understand those differences can help us appreciate each other. In the end, people are people, right?

For the interracial-dating-challenged, I will say that we who date interracially don't date someone because they are specifically not of our ethnic origin. It's not that we like to be with women who do not look like us and forget all about the women that have been there with us from the beginning. The bottom line is that we date someone we like, someone with common interests, or someone who just happens to not be of the same race.

Indulge me for a minute or two as I become the self-proclaimed, all-knowing Oracle of Delphi. I have learned that when you close yourself off to other races, you may miss out on an amazing person who may have been placed in your life at that particular time so you can learn something about yourself.

Some of us from the later generations have fewer issues with race than our parents and grandparents who grew up in a time of extreme racial unrest and bigotry. Sometimes, some of what they went through will manifest in their views of your relationships—even though they may deny having issues with interracial dating when asked.

All that you can hope for – with time, your family will become more accepting of them.

However, ultimately, it is your life. You have to live your life and be happy. The people in your life are going to have to get used to it. It is your decision to make – as Shakespeare wrote, "To thine own self, be true."

Since It Worked For Me, It Should Work For You

This common phrase does not necessarily always ring true in the realm of relationships. Men and women are very different beings, especially in the way we deal with certain situations. When arguments arise in my relationships, I tend to step away from the situation, take some time, and evaluate what has been said. I step away not because I want to avoid the conversation but I want to try to understand the other person's point of view which is quite difficult to do in the middle of a heated argument. Arguments can be so powerfully charged with emotion that you ignore the voice of reason because you are so committed to having your point—and only your point—understood.

Some people want to deal with issues immediately. However, that is only best if both of you communicate best in that fashion – and it is an issue of extreme importance or necessity. Some people say, "Every time we argue about something, it is of extreme importance." Think about the argument in hindsight. Was that really the case? After a cooling down period, sometimes people realize they have been arguing over the silliest things.

Forcing the other person to talk about issues, in my experience, will only cause them to rebel and resent you. They may shut down at the notion that you want to talk about something. A defensive attitude might be taken against any points you try to make—whether they realize your point is valid or not. Most importantly, you must understand how your partner feels as though they best handle disagreements. You may not agree with their method entirely but it may the best way for them to handle a situation until they see a better alternative.

I was in another long-distance relationship with a young lady that I was deeply in love with at the time. However, there were so many differences between us that eventually we decided it was better for us to be friends. The path to friendship meant taking different roads for each of us. The hurt and disappoint at that time that I felt was unlike anything I had ever experienced. I had taken the leap by giving my heart to someone I thought would be my wife. My future life consisted of *we*—not me. To see that come to an end was devastating.

She was the type of person that wanted to deal with issues immediately. She wanted to continue our "modified" relationship, although the status had changed, as if nothing had happened. When she called, I would not answer the phone. I would not e-mail, call, or have any type of communication with her for weeks at a time. She ultimately became very frustrated with me. At one point, she told me she was tired of trying to have a relationship with me and hoped that I had a nice life.

After many weeks, I began to speak to her over my computer's instant messenger periodically, but that was not enough for her. As she explained, she wanted to hear my voice. I explained that I had to make a separation from us as lovers, being committed, and talking about marriage, children, and growing old together to being friends and returning to the dating scene. She did not understand that I had to condition my mind and spirit to understand that we were not together anymore; in all likelihood, we would never be together.

The only way I could do that was to completely distance myself from her for a period of time and gradually, but less frequently, talk to her. Although it hurt her, frustrated her, and was hard for her to understand, I had to do it in order to deal with the separation and change in our relationship. Consequently, I know that it may not have been the absolute best way to handle a situation that arises in a relationship, but it is what I had to do in order to cope with losing her.

I gained some wisdom from this experience. I learned that you must allow the other person in your life the time they need to work through issues in their own way—and try to be supportive of them while they do. Being supportive and accommodating are essential to a relationship—even when you may not always understand why.

Miss You Like Crazy

L adies, have you ever dated someone for some time, but all of a sudden he does not want to come over as he normally does? Or maybe he tells you he has already eaten when you invite him to dinner or lunch just as you do every night. Or he does not answer his phone although he has already talked to you six times that day? When he does answer, and you ask what is wrong, does he have nothing to say and seem a bit agitated? If you are wondering why this seemingly unknown phenomenon may begin to happen in your relationship, I can tell you why these strange behaviors appear as seemingly from out of nowhere.

Ladies, are you ready for this one? This is a big one. Here we go. Ladies, we need the opportunity to miss you sometimes. Trust me when I tell you the adage absence makes the heart grow fonder is true. All we ask is that we have the opportunity to put it into practice sometimes.

When you call after we have talked four times within two hours and ask what we're doing, if it seems like we are not much of a participant in the conversation, it's probably because not much has changed in two hours. If we are spending every minute together with no breaks away from each other, the relationship can become stale. Men, like anyone else, need their time to decompress from the events of the day or week; sometimes that time does not involve being with our significant other.

Some women become overly sensitive when we say that we need our time to do what we want to do. Please do not take offense to that comment if it has ever been made to you. We are not going out to try to find the next woman in our life; we just need time to be individuals. One thing that must be understood is that, even though you are in a relationship with someone, you are still individuals who have certain separate interests. Those interests are an integral part of who people are; as long as it is not something that is detrimental to themselves or the relationship, let it be. Trying to take that time or hobby away—or coming between it—will only cause resentment, distance, and separation.

My parents have been married for thirty-nine years. As long as I can remember, I have known that my dad loves to fish. It is his passion and his release. I have come to the conclusion that he worked the graveyard shift at his plant for twenty-five years so he could get off in the mornings and go fishing. It has always been his way of releasing the stress in his life; it seems to put things back in focus for him. He can spend twelve hours or more on his boat if the fish are biting. The most beautiful part of his passion for fishing is that my mom understands that it is one of his loves in life. She does not try to get in the middle or test it because she knows that is one of his loves. She even has gone out on the water with him even though she does not fish. The tension occurs when those passions or personal time needs are tested even though the need for them may have been communicated early on in the relationship.

I once dated a lady, but I realized after a few weeks that she was someone who liked to talk on the phone a lot. I let her know that I was not that type of person. For me, the phone is a tool and not a recreation. One night, after we had talked about four times that day, she called again. She noticed that I did not have much to say to her. Over time, the conversation had moved from a flowing dialog to a trickling of occasional comments to keep the conversation alive. When she asked what was wrong, I again told her that I was not much of a telephone person.

I also had told her on previous occasions that I try not to converse, exist, or have any knowledge of the outside world when the Miami Heat, Duke Blue Devils, or Dallas Cowboys are on TV. To further drive my point home, I politely told her that my own mother does not call me or try to converse when those teams play because she knows that she will not have one ounce of my coherent attention.

The trial by fire came during the NBA Playoffs featuring The Miami Heat. This time I answered the phone because I had not talked to her all day. I wanted to hear from her because sometimes you just want to hear someone's voice. When she asked what I was doing, I told her that I was watching getting ready to the game and would call her once it was over. She tried to carry on a conversation, but I was noticeably distant. She asked me what was wrong again, and I said I was watching the game. She was a bit upset, but the game was something I had told her earlier in the week that would get my undivided attention.

On other occasions, she tried to have conversations, but the situation always had the same outcome. She continued to call and be upset when I did not answer—and I continued to watch the games. If you try to test your man's personal time, you may win the individual battle, but you will lose the war. You may get his attention for that moment, but he will pull away, feeling a bit smothered. Eventually, there will be distance. I guarantee that if you let us have those few moments of "me time," we will be spending the longer, more meaningful moments with you.

Patience Is A Virtue

Ladies, I have a confession about my brethren and me. From time to time when we begin a relationship with you, we act selfishly. Sometimes we act on things without consideration for how it may affect you and the way that you feel. I admit it. In the beginning of a relationship, we do it all the time. But on the flipside, this should be expected. It is nothing that you should indict him for doing. Why would I say such a thing? I'll tell you why.

These situations happen because of the basic nature of life. Oddly enough, it is a characteristic that I am quite sure happens in your life as well. People are creatures of habit; a man that has been single for a long time may still be in the habit of operating in the mind-set of a single person even though he is in a relationship with you.

Science tells us that when you develop a habit, certain things become somewhat instinctive. If we believe science in this case, then being single for a long time causes men to become selfish because they have only had to look out for *numero uno* and take care of themselves. When you are single, your life decisions primarily affect you. So therefore, the mind-set is somewhat singular in direction and focus. As with any habit, whether it is smoking, shopping, etc, it takes time to change those single life habits and develop the new habits of being in a relationship; time to understand and consider the emotions and wellbeing of your partner. Habits take time to develop and even longer to change and therein lies the reason why men may seem inconsiderate to you and your feelings at times even though they aren't trying to be that way. Changing from a single person's mind-set is not going to happen overnight. The best thing you can do is be patient with him. Know that he is going to revert back to those old habits from time to time because they are habitual by his formerly single nature. As time passes, those habits will diminish.

In the early stages of a relationship, don't set the high expectation level that he will always be the considerate, perfect boyfriend because he won't be. He is going to make mistakes in judgment that do not take your feelings into consideration, but please understand that these mistakes are not intentional.

Even if he has been in previous relationships—and you feel as though these are things he should already know—remember that if you don't practice something, you lose it. Give us the opportunity to relearn and reapply the skills that it takes to be in a relationship. In time, he will come around and develop the habits that it takes to sustain a healthy relationship with you.

When you see him acting as if he was single and you don't understand why, hopefully, you will have a better understanding now. Patience, by all means, is a virtue.

It's Not You, It's Her

Trust is one of the most essential ingredients for a healthy relationship, but it's frustrating as hell to see my some of my fellas in relationships with overbearing women. These women say that they trust their man completely, but they trip out when another woman looks at the guy. They become the judge, jury, and executioner of a man who had no control over the woman who looked or smiled at him as she passed by.

When the heated discussion starts about the smiling passerby, he says, "What's wrong? You don't trust me?" She says, "I trust you, baby. It is the other women I don't trust." What a bunch of bull! Be truthful with yourselves. In reality, these women don't trust their men. What they are really saying is that they don't think their man can control himself around other women and remain faithful to them. They are saying that if a woman makes advances at their man, they don't think he has the willpower to tell her that he is in a relationship—and happy in that relationship. It's as if they only trust him when they are with him because they can see what he is doing. And that, my most beautiful gender, is really the truth.

Give your man at least that much respect to know that he understands if he is in a relationship with you, then he is in a relationship with you—and only you. For women that fall in this category, the issues may be deeper than what they are letting on. It may be an issue of self-insecurity. Do some soul-searching to find out what insecurities make you feel this way. Whether it is from a past relationship or other reasons, address it. It will only help strengthen your relationship with the man in your life.

Trust, in my opinion, is something that not enough people really take the time to understand. Have you ever talked with your man and expected a jealous response, but his response was based on his total trust of you as his woman. When there was no hint of jealousy, it upset you. As crazy as it may seem, it is almost as if the possibility of distrust makes her feel more comfortable and secure. Want to figure out what that means?

I once dated a young lady that I trusted completely—and I mean completely. She did have a few male friends. The common denominator for her male friends is that I knew about them. She told me that these guy friends were not all former boyfriends. I believed what she said because I trusted her to tell me the truth. Amazing, isn't it? While we dated, she would travel back to her hometown occasionally and visit some of these friends while she was there. They would call her at times and, on one occasion, a mutual friend came to visit her while I was out of town on business. If I was out of town on business, she would call to tell me that she was going somewhere or that they were coming to visit her in Vegas for a weekend. Since I trusted her, I said it was fine.

One night in a heart-to-heart talk, I found out that she felt that I did not care about her as much as she thought I should because I did not get jealous when she would tell me that she was going somewhere for the weekend or someone was coming to see her for the weekend. It disturbed her that I always said okay and never had any objections. It was not that I did not care about her or felt nonchalant about our relationship. I trusted her because I was in a relationship with *her*. If she chose to do something to jeopardize our relationship, that was her cross to bear. I couldn't control that because I trusted her enough to do the right thing and respect me as the man in her life.

However, if I found out that there were indiscretions that took place, it would be over between us right then and there. As my one of my best friends would say, "I will give you enough rope to hang yourself." Eventually, any indiscretions will come to the light. You can't blame anyone but yourself if you choose to throw away the trust that has been given to you.

Absolute trust is a powerful, precious gift. When someone gives you complete trust, respect it and treat it as a gift.

Before anyone talks about trust, take the time to fully understand what complete trust means. Use my experience as a guideline for your own self-discovery into what trust really is.

I Am Not Him

L adies, here is a good bit of advice. Your girlfriend's man is not your man. Don't expect your man to do what her man does.

Let's say you have a girlfriend who is—or was—dating someone. You find out that he is not treating her fairly or doing the things that are expected in a relationship. Maybe he is being outright disrespectful and cheating on her. As much as you may dislike what is happening, please do not bring your girlfriend's issues and insecurities home and insert them into your relationship. It will only cause problems for you and your man because, as time goes on and accusations begin to mount, he will get tired of them and you may find yourself by yourself. Your man cannot change the things that have happened to your friend in her relationship. The best thing you can do in that is situation is support your friend when she needs it—and leave her home situation where it belongs: in her home.

Likewise, if there is something that your girlfriend's man does that is positive and you would like to see it happen in your relationship, don't expect it to miraculously show up in yours and then become upset with your man when it does not come to fruition. Why? It may not be in your man's makeup—or even know that it is something that you would like to see. Therefore, you have to discuss it with him. We are all individuals with different qualities and traits, but I can assure you that being able to read minds is *not* one of those traits. If we did have that ability, we would always seek relationship advice—and we would always get it right the first time around.

There Was A Life Before You

There is a double standard for the types of friends that men and women have during a relationship. I can't count the number of times I have heard women say that they have more guy friends than girl friends and that's the way it has always been because they just don't get along with other women because of the cattiness. So, if this is the case, explain why it is an issue if a man has more female friends than male friends? Don't the same rules apply? I would like to say they would, but we all know they don't. Here is a newsflash that may be hard to believe. All men have not slept with every female friend they have ever met or spent time with. Men are capable of platonic relationships just as much as women are—despite the notion that "the only female friends men have are the ones they haven't slept with yet."

What would you do if you and your man were walking down the street, he saw an old female friend, and she said hello. After they hugged, he introduced you to her and told you how they knew each other. You all make small talk and then move on about your seemingly merry way. Would you be upset with him? Would you be jealous? If you answered yes, please explain why. He had a life before you—a life that has spanned more years than the two of you have been together. Somewhere along the way, he may have met a few people. Lo and behold, some of them may have been women.

The jealousy stems from insecurity in your relationship. What it really comes down to is whether you trust your man as much as you say you do. His past life is his past life; if you are building something together, then you should focus on what you began building from the moment you met—and not on the life before you knew each other.

It would seem that it might be appreciated that he would introduce you to his female friend. Would that not suggest that there is absolutely nothing to hide about their relationship? What you should worry about is a situation where he does not introduce you to his female friends. That would be a more justified reason to question his intentions. Ladies, all we ask is that the same standard you have with your male friends is applied to our female friends.

Relationships Are?

During my relatively few years here on earth, I have found that a relationship can be many things and mean many different things to different people. Two people can be together physically without being in the same relationship mentally.

What is my interpretation of a relationship? I am sure it will be the same for some of you and markedly different for the rest of you.

For some reason, a relationship seems to be classified only as two people in a committed partnership with each other. Experience has led me—and other men—to believe that a single classification for a relationship paints the situation with too broad a brush.

Let's dig a little deeper and really analyze the word. Relationships come in many forms. The most common is a friendship, which most of us have created and experienced in our lifetime. Some last a long time, and some of them are fleeting. In any event, it is still a relationship. The true meaning of a relationship is the interaction between individuals who develop some type of bond through a common interest or ideal.

Likewise, friendship is a common word, but it probably is not looked at closely enough. Over the course of time, it has lost a bit of its value. I tell people that I can count my closest friends on my two hands and for the most part, that is the truth. A friend is someone who always has my best interests at heart, someone who is there in my time of need, someone I can talk to without fear of being judged, and someone who listens sometimes without giving advice. A friend is family—as much as if you were birthed by the same mother. To me, that is what constitutes a friend.

Relationships can take on another form—a relationship that can cause many misunderstandings. I am talking about the notorious "friendships with understandings." I have observed —and been a part of—relationships that have had this meaning. This type of relationship must have the ultimate level of communication and honesty to know if you should allow yourself to become a part of it.

This type of relationship is most commonly characterized by two people who enjoy each other's company. They may go out for an occasional dinner, but they are not at a point in their lives where they want to make the commitment—and put in the work—to have a committed relationship between the two of them. They do, however, have a physical attraction to each other. This is the type of relationship that needs the occasional emotional pit stops to gauge the level of feelings between the two people involved. Not doing so can lead to needless ruined friendships.

Too often in this type of relationship, we don't take a true inventory of who we are and what we are willing to accept. In this relationship, you have to come to terms with the possibility that the person that you are involved with may decide to see someone else at the same time they are seeing you. The question is whether you can deal with that. Be truthful. Ask yourself how you would feel. Remove the physical attraction from the equation in order to truly evaluate your feelings. If there is any hint that you may be upset by that person dating someone else while they are seeing you, then this is probably not the right relationship for you. The bottom line is that you have to know what you want out of it—and what you are willing to accept. Once you have defined what that limit is, be true to yourself and live by it.

A Reason, A Season, Or A Lifetime

Why does someone who you think is supposed to be in your life forever suddenly leave it? Why does a person that you would love to have a relationship with only remain a platonic friend?

People come into our lives for a season, a reason, or a lifetime. These wise words refer to the length of time that people stay into our lives. No one you meet is by circumstance. I truly believe that each person that spends a certain amount of time in our lives was meant to teach us something about life or ourselves and vice versa.

I believe that for every one of us who are meant to be married, every relationship that we have been in, whether it is good or bad, was designed to teach us something and prepare us for our soul mate.

It could have been a lesson on how you want to be and should be treated. It could have been a lesson on how to treat the person you are to love—or what you want in the perfect companion. Each relationship brings us closer to knowing who Ms. or Mr. Right really is for us.

As sure as there is a sun in the sky, if you live long enough, you will have many relationships. They may be lost friendships or someone you dated that makes you wonder why that person was ever in your life—especially if it was a relationship where it seemed that everything was going well until something separated you from that person. For some, it could take a lifetime to figure these things out; some we will never figure out.

Life is one big lesson designed to teach us how to be the best human we can be. This progression does not happen all at once because, at certain stages in our lives, we may not be ready to handle the lesson. It may not be the most important life lesson we need to learn at that time. It is my belief that God delivers his lessons for us through the lives of people and, hopefully at the end, we get it.

One of my biggest lessons occurred a few years ago when I was at a very low point in my life. My first project assignment in Florida ended, and I had no job for more than a year. I could not find one no matter how hard I searched. If you were to look at my résumé, I had the credentials for the positions to which I was applying, but I could not even get a phone call from anyone.

Spiritually, I knew there was a massive void in my life, but when I look back at it, my belief in anything good for my life had wavered and diminished. I used to attend church regularly, but I had stopped going. I knew I needed to regain that connection, but I wondered what the point was.

During this time, as He would have it, I met a young lady named Linda. We hit it off very well. This young lady went against every dating principle that I had ever lived by. I was not looking for a relationship, but she was. I had said that I would not date a woman with children, and she had two. Normally, that would have caused me to hit the door running, but I stuck around for some reason.

The thing that I found interesting about her is that she was so spiritual and had such an unwavering faith. She was always talking about the wonders of God or going to church; during the week, on Sunday, she was always asking me to go with her. I fought it for a long time, but the visible testimony of her life could not be denied. Her faith, despite being a single mother with two children, allowed her to believe that God would take care of everything she needed. I was a witness to some things that happened in her life that, to this day, I still can't explain. Everything always seemed to work out for her.

I began to see that I had to make a change in my life. I began to reconnect with God. Over time, things in my life began to change; the more I built my belief, the better I felt about life.

As fate would have it, after about a year of dating, I accepted a job opportunity that I had always wanted. The position allowed me to travel and work away from an office. The problem was that I would have to stop dating her because we both knew that she was a woman who needed her man there. Being gone ten months of the year was not going to work in our situation. It hurt so badly because I thought this may have been the woman I was going to marry—and I had grown to love her little girls. I was having a hard time letting go of the relationship, but we both knew it was the right thing at the time.

The frustrating part was that I could not figure out why, once again, someone that I had deeply loved was being taken out of my life. After struggling with it for months, the answer I was looking for came to me. The lesson that I was supposed to learn while I was with her had come to an end. The purpose for her being in my life at that time was to help me regain my spirituality with God. For that, I am most thankful.

Do you want more proof of how people being placed in your life for a period of time can affect not only your life but the lives of others? When I lived in Charlotte, North Carolina, I had always said that I wanted to live in Florida someday. By what some would call chance, I received an e-mail from a job recruiter wanting to know if I was interested in a business analyst position in Florida. Since it was a random e-mail, I almost deleted it, but I decided to respond.

A few days later, the recruiter called to say that the hiring manager wanted to conduct an interview over the phone—and possibly fly me out for a face-to-face interview. The phone interview went very well and before the end of the week, I was on a plane to Florida. I had the interview on a Thursday, and I was hired that same day. I was expected to be packed up and in Florida to start work that following Monday. What a whirlwind in the span of a week! I was in a new city, knowing only my cousin, her husband and their kids. I was having a little trouble adjusting to everything that was going on.

This is where the story really gets interesting, and it can be nothing short of divine intervention. As much as the next two incidents may seem as though they have no connection, bear with me, and you will see the infinite wisdom of God.

One night while I was out on the town, I met a young lady named Cat. She worked for a cosmetics company at the mall, and she told me to stop by to say hello. We hit it off pretty well and developed a friendship. A few weeks prior to knowing Cat, I had walked past that same store and seen a statuesque, attractive young lady. I had called one of my best friends, Scott immediately to tell him about her since I thought she was his type of girl. I also told him that he would love it in my new city, and he should visit soon. Jokingly, I told him he would like it so much that he would want to move to Florida.

As fate would have it, my manager had another position available for our team. She asked if I knew anyone who would be interested in applying. I offered Scott's name, and he was hired as well.

A month later, Scott moved to town. That same week, Cat's work was having a get together at a local restaurant, and she invited us. We accepted. I told her that I thought Scott would hit it off very well with Kim (Ms. Statuesque). On the day of the party, I met Cat at the restaurant. Kim was there, but Scott wasn't. I tried to call him, but he would not answer his phone. I called and called and called, but he did not pick up. Little did I know that Cat had told Kim that Scott was coming; when he did not show up, well, you know the rest of the story if you know any red-blooded American woman. She was not impressed.

After the party, I went back to the apartment and told Scott that the girl I wanted him to meet was there. I asked why he hadn't answered the phone. He said, "I don't know. I just didn't feel like going."

It seemed as if all had been lost for Scott and Kim, but that's where divine intervention comes in. Cat decided that she was going to throw a dinner and pool party at her townhouse, and she invited us again. I told Scott that he was going—and that he was going to ride with me. This way, he had no way out. We walked in the house and when he saw Kim, he looked at me as if to say, "Man, what was I thinking?" I looked back at him as if to say, "Exactly."

After dinner, we all went over to the pool. Kim and Scott hit it off very well and exchanged information but unfortunately, Kim would soon be moving back to Hawaii. When she finally moved, they remained friends and kept in touch throughout.

After Kim moved, Scott started dating another young lady at our work. Over the course of the next year or so, things between the two of them did not work out, but Scott remained friends with his ex's best friend.

His relationship with Kim continued to grow, and it developed into something much more. Eventually, Kim moved back to Florida to be with Scott.

In the midst of all of this change, there was a big change in my life too. Once again, I was without steady work. When my contract ended, I had problems finding more work.

As the Divine One would have it, Scott and Kim were invited to a cookout that his ex's best friend was having. There he met a gentleman that was a manager for a very large construction wholesale distribution company. That gentleman was his ex-girlfriend's best friend's brother. His group conducted all of the onsite training, system implementations, and ongoing support for the company. He and Scott talked about careers, and he offered a position on his team to Scott. Scott could not accept the offer because he had just found new employment. However, Scott said his roommate, namely me, might be interested. I sent my résumé in to the manager, and to make a long story short, I have worked for that company for the past six years.

If I had not gotten the initial job recruiter e-mail, Scott would not have met Kim— who I am proud to say is now his wife. And if Scott did not date his ex and meet her best friend, he would have never met her brother—and I would not have the career that I have always dreamed about. Now, tell me who else but the Divine One would know all of this and be able to put all of these lives together at the precise moments in time?

On the surface, these seemingly unrelated, but ultimately connected, stories show that no moment or relationship in life is insignificant. Maybe there was a lesson to learn—or you may have been the medium to connect other lives in some way that may or may not be revealed at that time. Nothing happens by coincidence—nothing.

In the End

So what does all this mean? Is this a judgment against all women? Not in the least. Is this the definitive literary work on relationships that will fix all relationship issues between men and women? Hardly.

However, my sincere hope is that this book has given some insight into the minds of men and some of the things that we discuss and struggle with in relationships. It is important for us to have our point of view heard and more importantly understood.

I hope that this book is a catalyst that will spark a discussion between men and women, creating a dialogue of how important it is to communicate on a level that is respectful to all of us. I hope it shows how important it is to effectively listen to what is being said—and not what either person wants to hear. This catalyst will reinforce the most important ingredient in any successful relationship: communication. Without communication, there is no understanding; without understanding, there is no relationship.

Live more. Love more. Be blessed.

Printed in the United States
By Bookmasters